Keepsake Crafts
FOR GRANDMA AND ME

BY MEGAN HEWES BUTLER

ILLUSTRATIONS BY FRANCESCA DE LUCA

ODD DOT  NEW YORK

Table of Contents

CHOOSE A CRAFT AND
SPEND TIME TOGETHER!

Introduction

Dear Grandma and Grandkiddo,

Welcome! I'm so glad you're both here. In your hands you hold a guide to minutes, hours, and days you can spend sharing memories—and creating new ones—across generations. Make crafts together that help you dream, connect, play, create, share, and remember. When you're finished, cherish these keepsakes or give them as gifts to spread the love.

Inside these pages you'll find:

TIME TOGETHER ICONS

Use these time icons to help you select a project that fits your time together. Feel free to work at your own pace— these are just estimations to help you plan.

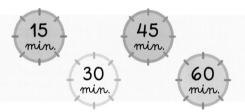

MOMENTS TO TREASURE

Use this heart icon to cue you in to places where you can stay in the moment together—whether taking a nature walk side by side, drawing your dreams, or collaboratively making up stories. These are moments to simply enjoy being together.

SPECIAL MATERIALS

Use this star icon to know which projects use special materials (printed cardstock or stickers) from the back of the book.

Use the features above to help choose your first project. When you finish a craft, don't forget to sign and date the other side. Then share smiles creating two wonderful things together— a keepsake craft and a special memory!

Yours,

Megan Hewes Butler

Together Forever Jar

Remember today's adventures together with memories sealed up tight.

TIME TOGETHER: **45** min.

GATHER THESE ITEMS:

☆ Cardstock from page 63
- Scissors
- Jar or container (4-cup [1 liter] size or larger)
- Small photographs (one of each of you or one together)
- Glue
- Drawing tools like crayons, colored pencils, or markers
- Non-living outdoor items (see step #1)

LET'S GET STARTED:

♡ 1. Go on a nature walk together and collect non-living items in your jar. Look for sand, pebbles, seeds, shells, twigs, pine cones, pine needles, bark, and more.

(Tip: Do this activity on a special day, like a trip or event somewhere together, or on a regular afternoon in the park or backyard.)

2. Work together to arrange the items in the bottom of your jar. Make a scene by pouring in the sand or pebbles first. Then arrange the larger items, like twigs or bark. Place in the smaller items, like seeds or shells, last.

3. Cut out the photographs of the two of you. Stick them down into the jar. (Stand them upright, or use a little glue on the backs to attach them to an item or to the back of the jar.)

4. Cut out the banners, signs, and bubbles from the sheet of cardstock.

5. Fill in the cutouts with the date, location, thoughts, quotes, jokes, drawings, and more.

6. Add the cutouts to the jar. Place them down into the base, or add glue to the backs. You can even glue some to the outside of the jar!

7. Display your jar where you can talk about the special things that you remember. Start a collection of jars with more events, places, and time spent together—all sealed up tight!

Love You Everywhere Guidepost

Create a guidepost of where your favorite memories have taken you.

TIME TOGETHER: **45** min.

PLUS A FEW DAYS TO DRY

GATHER THESE ITEMS:

- ☆ Cardstock from page 65
- Scissors
- Drawing tools like crayons, colored pencils, or markers
- Stick or wooden dowel about as long as your forearm
- Wax paper
- Air-dry clay
- Glue
- City map or online mapping tool
- Pencil
- Optional: A few sheets of colored construction paper

For other crafts with air-dry clay, check out *Friendship Necklaces* or *Little Hands to Hold*

LET'S GET STARTED:

1. Cover your workspace with wax paper.

2. Roll an egg-sized amount of air-dry clay into a ball, then press it down flat on your work surface. (Tip: Add just a little bit of water to your fingertips to perfect any cracks or sticky areas.)

3. Press your stick into the middle of the clay so that it stands straight up.

4. Use the tip of a sharp pencil to carve the cardinal directions (N, E, S, W) into the clay evenly around the stick.

5. Follow the instructions on the clay's package and allow it to dry. This may take a few days.

6. While your clay is drying, cut out the arrows from the sheet of cardstock and fold each one in half.

7. Talk about places where the two of you have memories together: your homes, homes of other family members, special trips, or places you both like to visit. Write the name of each place on its own arrow. (Tip: If you run out of arrows you can cut more from your own paper.)

8. Use a map or online mapping tool to search for the location of your first place. How many miles away is it from where you are now? Write the number of miles on the arrow next to the name.

9. Check your map to see which direction your first place is in relation to where you are now—north, northeast, northwest, or another direction. Open up the arrow and place glue on the inside. Fold it over the stick and close it to seal the glue. Turn it to face the correct direction.

10. Repeat steps 8 and 9 until all of your arrows are placed on the stick, and allow the glue to dry.

11. Display your guidepost and continue to add your new adventures and special places!

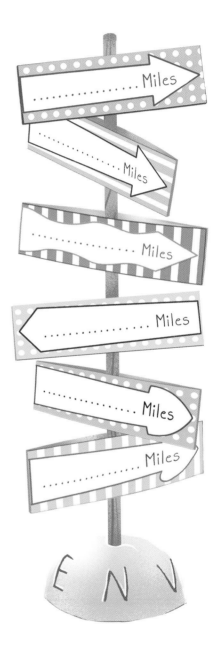

Favorite Things Mobile

Create a balance sculpture to hang
your favorite memories.

LET'S GET STARTED:

1. Go on a hunt inside and outside your home
   to collect small items that remind you both
   of your memories together.
   You may find:

   - Notecards you've sent or received

   - Artwork

   - Photographs

   - Small toys

   - Items from nature, like pine cones,
     dried flowers, or shells

   - Decorative items, like pom-poms, bows,
     buttons, or beads

2. Cut 8 pieces of string that are about as long
   as your grandkiddo's arm. Then cut two of
   the pieces in half. (You can cut more later if
   you need.)

3. Tie your longest piece of string around both
   ends of your longest stick. Place your stick,
   hanging from the string, on a doorknob or
   other hook near where you are working.

TIME TOGETHER: 45 min.

GATHER THESE ITEMS:

- At least 3 short sticks, disposable
  chopsticks, or pencils
- Hole punch
- String or yarn
- Scissors
- Small memorable items (see step #1)

4. Tie another piece of string around the middle of your second stick, then repeat with another piece of string and your last stick.

5. Tie the freestanding sticks each onto an end of your hanging stick.

6. Work together to tie your collection of small items onto your remaining strings.

Some items can be wrapped around a few times with a knot, while others may need a hole punch. Add an item at the end or in the middle of a piece of string. (Tip: Adding several items in a row on a string will add variety to your mobile.)

7. Tie the strings of items onto the sticks. You can add them to the longest stick or a shorter stick. Move each string right and left to balance out your mobile.
(Tip: If your mobile is too heavy on any side, try untying a string of items and moving it to the other side.)

8. Hang your mobile and continue to add (and balance!) new memories over time.

WRAP YOUR STICKS FULLY WITH STRING TO ADD MORE COLOR TO YOUR MOBILE!

Little Hands to Hold

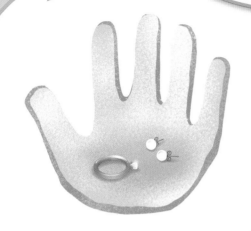

The little hands you love to hold can hold the little things you love.

For other crafts with air-dry clay, check out Friendship Necklaces or Love You Everywhere Guidepost

TIME TOGETHER: **60** **min.**

PLUS A FEW DAYS TO DRY

GATHER THESE ITEMS:

- Air-dry clay
- Wax paper
- Toothpick
- 2 small bowls with rounded bottoms
- Clear spray sealer
- Optional: 2 balloons

LET'S GET STARTED:

1. Cover your workspace with wax paper.

2. Divide a softball-sized ball of air-dry clay into halves, then knead each piece.

3. Press and roll each ball of clay into a flat disc about ½" (1 cm) thick. Use your palms to smooth out the surfaces.

4. Ask your grandkiddo to place an open hand on each disc. Trace around each hand with a toothpick.

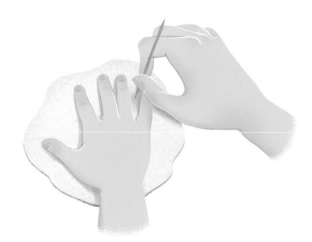

5. Remove both hands, then use the toothpick to press around the outlines through the clay to cut them out.

6. Smooth out any rough edges with your fingers. (Tip: Add just a little bit of water to your fingertips to perfect any cracks or sticky areas.)

7. Place both bowls upside down, then lay a clay hand on the bottom of each bowl.

8. Gently press down so that the hands curve around the bowl. (Tip: The best results come from bowls with no lip or seam on the bottom. As an alternative, place a balloon in each bowl to round the clay on.)

9. Follow the instructions on the clay's package to allow the hands to dry, usually about 3 days. Take them off the bowls and flip them over halfway through the drying time.

10. **(Grandmas only!)** In a safe location, follow the instructions on the spray sealer and cover each hand completely. Allow time for them to dry.

11. Display your little hands and use them to store jewelry, coins, or other small keepsakes.

COMPARE THE SIZES AND SHAPES OF YOUR HANDS—HOW ARE THEY THE SAME AND HOW ARE THEY DIFFERENT?

Where We Go Together Map

Make a shared map to weave your travels together.

TIME TOGETHER: 45 min.

GATHER THESE ITEMS:

- Empty bulletin board (larger works best)
- 10 or more pushpins
- Paper
- Drawing tools like crayons, colored pencils, or markers
- 2 pairs of scissors—1 for you and 1 for your grandkiddo
- 2 colors of yarn

LET'S GET STARTED:

1. Share stories about the past week: Where did you each go around your homes and neighborhoods? School? Work? The library? The park? A friend's home?

2. Draw and label pictures of each place you identified on a piece of paper. (Make sure to include your homes!)

3. Cut out your drawn pictures.

4. Place the pictures on your bulletin board and move them around to make a map. Which locations are close together? Which are far apart? When your map is complete, use pushpins to hold each location in place. (Tip: To help with the next steps, push each pin in as far as it will go.)

5. Choose a color of yarn for your grandkiddo and a different color for you. Cut a piece from each color that's about as tall as your grandkiddo.

6. Tie one end of your grandkiddo's yarn around the pushpin at their home. Tie one end of your yarn to the pushpin at your home. (They may even be the same home!)

7. Talk about the first place each of you went. (If you can't remember where you went in order, that's okay! Just choose one of the places you remember.) Pull your yarn to that location and wrap it once around the pushpin to hold it in place. Continue talking through each of your days and moving your yarns around the map you created.

8. When you are finished, notice: Where did you go together? Where did you each go the most?

Poem for Your Pocket

Give the gift of a pocket poem to someone you love.

TIME TOGETHER: **30 min.**

GATHER THESE ITEMS:

- 2 sheets of paper
- Drawing tools like crayons, colored pencils, or markers
- Scissors
- Tape
- ☆ Optional: "Use-anywhere stickers" from page 95

LET'S GET STARTED:

1. Fold the sheets of paper in half, then draw a large half heart starting at the fold of each sheet.

2. Cut out the half hearts and unfold them so you have two full hearts. (Tip: You can also trace and then cut out the heart shape on the inside back cover of this book.)

3. ♡ Work together to write a poem on each heart. An acrostic poem is one type you can try:

    G RANDMA
    R EADS BOOKS WITH ME
    A LWAYS GIVES ME HUGS
    N IBBLES ON CHOCOLATE
    D ANCES EVERY DAY
    M AKES THE BEST PANCAKES
    A ND LOVES ME VERY MUCH

    * Write your own name, or think of who you would like to give your poem to. Write their name vertically down the left-hand side, one letter on top of the other.

    * Write the same name again next to the first letter as the first line of the poem.

    * For all of the other letters of the name, write a word or a sentence that describes the person.

4. Decorate the backs of your hearts.

5. Fold in both side flaps on each heart. (There should be just enough space in the middle to fit your finger.)

6. Turn each heart upside down. Fold the bottom up to the top of the folded-in side flaps.

7. Fold down each top and seal it with a piece of tape or a sticker. Give your pocket poem away to share your love!

Mini Notes to Cherish

Design mini love notes together to mail when you are apart.

2. Place the notecard in the middle of a sheet of cardstock and ask your grandkiddo to trace around its edges.

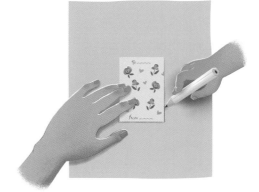

TIME TOGETHER: **30 min.**

GATHER THESE ITEMS:

☆ Cardstock from page 67
● Scissors
● Drawing tools like crayons, colored pencils, or markers
● Glue
● 2 or more sheets of cardstock or thick paper

3. Place your finger at the bottom edge of the notecard and slide it up. Ask your grandkiddo to trace the new top rectangle.

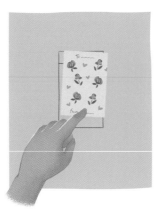

LET'S GET STARTED:

1. Select and cut out a notecard from the cardstock on page 67.

4. Place your finger on the bottom left and right corners of the rectangle and draw two marks.

5. Slide the left edge of your notecard over to the right mark and ask your grandkiddo to trace the new rectangle. Repeat to trace with the left mark.

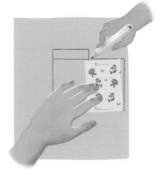

6. Place 2 fingers at the top edge and slide down the card. Ask your grandkiddo to trace the last rectangle at the bottom.

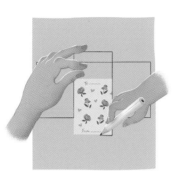

7. After your envelope template looks like this, cut around the outer edges.

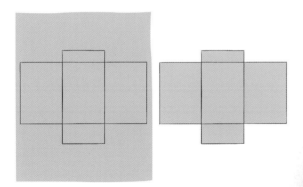

8. Take turns folding and creasing each flap.

9. Place a strip of glue along the top of a longer flap. Fold the other longer flap on top of it and press it down until secure.

10. Place a line of glue on the inside of the top flap and press it down until secure. (Tip: Cut the edges of this flap and the bottom flap for a fancier touch.)

11. Write and draw a message on your notecard.

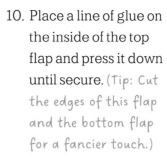

12. Place the notecard inside the envelope and glue the last flap closed.

13. Repeat the steps to make a second envelope together.

14. These tiny notecards (3½" x 5" or 9 cm x 13 cm) are the smallest allowable by the USPS. Put regular stamps on the envelopes and drop them in the mail to keep in touch when you are apart!

Rolling Conversations

Keep the conversation rolling with this special sharing dice.

TIME TOGETHER: **30 min.**

PLUS 30 MINUTES TO DRY

GATHER THESE ITEMS:

☆ Cardstock from page 69
● Scissors
● Glue
● Drawing tools like crayons, colored pencils, or markers

LET'S GET STARTED:

1. Cut out the dice template from your sheet of cardstock.

2. Get creative! In each of the 6 empty boxes, work together to brainstorm and draw a picture prompt about your favorite game, place, sport, animal, toy, etc.

3. Place the decorated side facedown and fold in the numbered tabs.

4. Flip over the dice template and fold along each of the dotted lines.

5. Add glue to all the tabs.

6. Starting with tab #1, press each tab into place with its matching number to assemble the dice.

7. When the dice is dry, roll and share together!

MAKE ANOTHER DICE WITH DIFFERENT THINGS TO TALK ABOUT, LIKE: "IF YOU COULD GO ANYWHERE, HAVE ANY SUPERPOWER, BE ANY AGE, CHANGE ANY RULE . . . WHAT WOULD YOU DO?" OR: "WHAT DO YOU WANT TO BE, SEE, LEARN, OR DO?"

Warm and Fuzzy Letters

Use colorful yarn and cardboard to share a warm and fuzzy message.

TIME TOGETHER: **45 min.**

GATHER THESE ITEMS:

- Leftover cardboard pieces (any shape and size)
- Pencil
- Scissors
- Masking tape
- Yarn (any color)
- Optional: Small items like buttons, small bells, pine cones, or dried pasta

LET'S GET STARTED:

1. Together, choose one or more letters to craft: This could be the first letter of your name, your initials, or a short message.

2. Draw each letter on a flat piece of cardboard. Make each letter about the same height (around 1 foot [30½ cm] tall is a good place to start). Then cut them out.

3. Tear 10 short pieces of tape and place them on the edge of your table or work surface for easy access.

4. Ask your grandkiddo to stand up tall, then measure and cut 5 pieces of yarn about as tall as they are.

5. Help your grandkiddo tape an end of the first piece of yarn to the back of the first cardboard letter.

6. Tightly wrap the yarn around and around the cardboard letter. When the yarn is done, use another piece of tape to secure it on the back of the letter.

7. Repeat steps 5 and 6 with more pieces of yarn until each letter is complete. (You may need to prepare more pieces of tape and yarn.)

8. Display your letters to share your warm and fuzzy message.

USE STRING OR TAPE TO ATTACH BUTTONS, SMALL BELLS, PINE CONES, OR DRIED PASTA SHAPES!

Friendship Necklaces

Wear your love close to your heart with these heart-shaped necklaces!

GATHER THESE ITEMS:

TIME TOGETHER: 60 min.

PLUS A FEW DAYS TO DRY

- Wax paper
- Air-dry clay
- Toothpick
- Acrylic or tempera paint
- 2 paintbrushes
- Clear spray sealer
- Scissors
- 3 colors of satin rattail cord (or embroidery floss), 1mm to 2mm thick

For other crafts with air-dry clay, check out Love You Everywhere Guidepost or Little Hands to Hold

LET'S GET STARTED:

1. Cover your work surface with wax paper.

2. Break off and knead a golf ball–sized piece of air-dry clay.

3. Roll the ball of clay and press it into a disc $1/3$" ($8/10$ cm) in diameter.

4. Use your toothpick to gently scratch around the shape of a heart. For a small necklace, aim for the size of a quarter. Or, aim for the size of a golf ball, or larger!
   (Tip: If you don't like the heart shape you scratched, press the clay to make it smooth and draw again.)

5. Use the toothpick to press around the outline through the clay to cut it out.

6. Use the toothpick to divide the heart in half and add a hole in the top of each piece. Wiggle the toothpick around to make sure that the holes go all the way through and are large enough for your cord.

7. Smooth out any rough edges with your fingers. Add just a little bit of water to your fingertips to perfect any cracks or sticky areas.

8. Follow the instructions on the clay's package to allow the heart halves to dry, usually about 3 days. Flip them over halfway through the drying time. Use the toothpick to wiggle the 2 holes again from the back to make sure they are large enough for your cord.

9. When the heart halves are dry, place them on your wax paper and paint them. Decorate a half of the heart for the other person.

10. **(Grandmas only!)** In a safe location, follow the instructions on the spray sealer and cover each half of the heart completely. Allow time for them to dry.

11. Cut 3 pieces of cord for each of you. Each person's cords should be longer than one arm, or long enough to make a necklace that loops over your head.

12. Thread the 3 pieces of cord through each half of the heart, then braid the strings!

13. Tie them closed, loop them over your heads, and wear them to showcase your friendship!

MAKE ANOTHER NECKLACE WITH A DIFFERENT SHAPE—A RAINBOW, CLOUD, OR ICE CREAM SUNDAE.

Shadow Silhouettes

Use light and shadow to record a lasting memory of your grandkiddo.

TIME TOGETHER: **45 min.**

GATHER THESE ITEMS:

- A sheet each of black paper and white paper
- Chair
- Desk lamp or bright reading lamp
- Tape
- 2 pairs of scissors—1 for you and 1 for your grandkiddo
- Drawing tools like crayons, colored pencils, or markers
- Glue

LET'S GET STARTED:

1. Ask your grandkiddo to draw a pattern on the white paper. They can repeat shapes, colors, pictures, or even scribbles.

2. While they are making their pattern, set up your shadow-drawing station:

   ★ Place a chair sideways next to a blank wall space.

   ★ Set up your lamp so that it points roughly where your grandkiddo's head will be.

   ★ Tape the black sheet of paper where the light hits the wall.

   ★ Dim or turn off the other lights in the room.

3. Once your station is ready, ask your grandkiddo to sit in the chair so their shadow silhouette is against the wall. Adjust the lamp and paper until you can see their silhouette on the paper. (Tip: Play music, sing together, or use a stuffed animal to help your grandkiddo sit in the chair for a few minutes.)

4. Trace your grandkiddo's silhouetted head and shoulders onto the paper.

5. Ask your grandkiddo to continue working on their pattern while you remove the black paper from the wall.

6. Carefully cut out the silhouette and glue it onto the patterned paper.

7. Frame and display your keepsake silhouette.

CREATE A SET OF SHADOW ART BY LETTING YOUR GRANDKIDDO MAKE YOUR SILHOUETTE!

Favorite Things Pencil Toppers

Keep memories of your favorite things "write" with you.

TIME TOGETHER: **15 min.**

GATHER THESE ITEMS:

☆ Cardstock from page 71
☆ "Use-anywhere stickers" from page 95
- 2 pairs of scissors—1 for you and 1 for your grandkiddo
- 3 or more pencils
- Drawing tools like crayons, colored pencils, or markers
- Optional: Photographs of friends and family

LET'S GET STARTED:

1. Talk together about your favorite things—what makes you both happy? What reminds you of each other and your time together?

2. Cut out the shapes from your sheet of cardstock.

3. Color the shapes however you like.

4. Pinch a shape in half with your fingers and make a small cut on both dots, then repeat for the other shapes.

5. Slide each shape onto a pencil, up to the eraser end.

6. Use your pencils together to draw and write, or give the toppers as personalized gifts!

BE CREATIVE AND MAKE MORE PENCIL TOPPERS WITH DIFFERENT SHAPES—OR EVEN PHOTOGRAPHS!

Bookmark Heart

Design bookmarks to hold close to your heart.

TIME TOGETHER: **15** min.

GATHER THESE ITEMS:

- 2 pieces of square paper (at least 8½" x 8½", or 21½ cm x 21½ cm)
- Scissors
- Drawing tools like crayons, colored pencils, or markers
- "Use-anywhere stickers" from page 95

LET'S GET STARTED:

1. Work side by side with your own papers: Fold your paper in half to form a triangle.

2. Fold your triangle in half again to make a crease. Then unfold it so it lies flat.

3. Fold down the front sheet of paper until the top point touches the bottom edge of the triangle.

4. Fold and crease the right and left points to meet in the middle. Then unfold them.

5. Fold up the right point until it touches the top of your triangle. Then use the crease you made to fold the top half down into the pocket. Repeat with the left point.

6. On the pocketed side, draw 2 equally round shapes across the top of the triangle. Then cut along the drawn shapes.

7. Flip over the hearts. Write and draw on the fronts, or add stickers from page 95.

8. Share your love of reading and explore a story together with your bookmarks!

Treasure Pockets

Store treasured mementos nearby in these handmade wall pockets.

  15 min.

GATHER THESE ITEMS:

 Cardstock from page 73
- Scissors
- Clear or decorative tape
- Removable double-sided tape (or wall-safe mounting squares)

LET'S GET STARTED:

1. Cut out the 2 treasure pockets from your sheet of cardstock.

2. Fold your first pocket in along the dotted lines. Then open up the pocket.

3. Tear off a piece of clear tape a few inches long and place it face-out on the marking.

4. Press the other half of the pocket against the tape to seal the pocket together. (The tape should now be on the inside.)

5. Repeat steps 2 through 4 with your second pocket.

6. Place strips of the removable double-sided tape on the 2 back upper corners of each pocket, then attach the pockets to a wall.

7. Go on a hunt together to find treasures and memories to fill your special wall pockets!

Hanging Art Globes

Cut, fold, and form 3-D paper globes to showcase your artwork masterpieces.

TIME TOGETHER: **60** min.

GATHER THESE ITEMS:

- Round cup or jar (with about a 3" or 7½ cm opening)
- Drawings, paintings, or other 2-D artwork for cutting (plain construction paper will also work)
- Pencil
- 2 pairs of scissors—1 for you and 1 for your grandkiddo
- A piece of white paper
- Glue
- 20 paper clips
- Optional: Hole punch, string

LET'S GET STARTED:

1. Work together: Turn your cup upside down on a piece of artwork, then trace a circle around the cup. Repeat this 19 times to make 20 different circles of art.

2. Cut out all the circles you traced. (Tip: Sign the artist's name on some of the circles or write other messages on the art!)

3. Trace a circle on the sheet of white paper. Line up the circle you traced on the template below.

 TRIANGLE TEMPLATE FOR STEP #3.

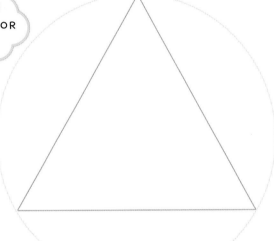

4. Trace the triangle from the template on top of your circle, then cut it out.

5. Lay the triangle template on top of one of your artwork circles and fold up the 3 side flaps. Work together to repeat this for all 20 circles.

6. Line up 10 of your folded circles in a row so the triangles form a pattern: one pointing up, one pointing down, etc.

7. Glue the touching flaps together. (Tip: If needed, use a paper clip on each glued flap to hold them tight while they dry.)

8. Stand up the glued circles like a fence, then glue the 2 outside flaps together to form a ring.

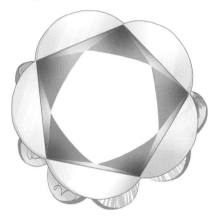

9. Line up your remaining circles to form 2 separate stars of 5 circles each.

10. Glue the touching flaps in each star.

11. Line up one star on top of your ring and glue the touching flaps.

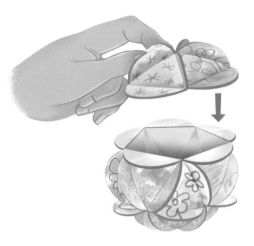

12. Flip the globe over and glue on the other star where the flaps touch.

13. Use a hole punch and string to add a hanging loop to your globe.

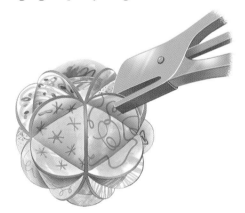

14. Hang your globe to showcase your artwork in a new (round) way!

Celebrate Every Day Garland

String up your special memories to celebrate every day.

TIME TOGETHER: 45 min.

GATHER THESE ITEMS:

- 5 or more photographs of yourselves, friends and family, and memories together
- 2 pairs of scissors—1 for you and 1 for your grandkiddo
- 3 or more colored sheets of paper
- Drawing tools like crayons, colored pencils, or markers
- Hole punch
- Yarn or string
- Tape
- Optional: Old tickets, postcards, pieces of artwork, dried pasta, or large beads

LET'S GET STARTED:

1. Choose a shape for your garland together—you can choose a triangle, circle, heart, square, or your own shape. Draw and cut out a shape, about the size of your hand, from your paper.

2. Use your cut-out shape as a template: trace it 5 more times on your other colors of paper. Then cut out all the shapes, to make 6 in all, and decorate them.

3. Use the hole punch to make 2 holes across the top of each shape and each photograph.

4. Cut a piece of string about twice as tall as your grandkiddo.

5. Weave the string through each hole in the shapes and photographs. Add optional items as you go: old tickets, postcards, pieces of artwork, dried pasta, or large beads.

6. Move the shapes and items along the string to space them out. Add a small piece of tape to the back of each item to hold it in place.

7. Hang up your garland to celebrate every day!

GARLANDS MAKE GREAT GIFTS FOR ALL OF YOUR LOVED ONES!

24

Family Handprint Tree

Get together to make a family tree—and see how it grows!

TIME TOGETHER: **30 min.**

PLUS A FEW HOURS TO DRY

GATHER THESE ITEMS:

- ☆ Cardstock from page 75
- Sheet of white or light-colored paper (at least 11" x 17", or 28 cm x 43 cm)
- Pencil or pen
- Scissors
- Glue
- Finger paint or tempera paint in various colors
- Paintbrush
- Large plate or tray

LET'S GET STARTED:

1. Cut out the tree trunk and other labels from the sheet of cardstock.

2. Glue the tree trunk a few inches up from the bottom edge of your paper.

3. Place dollops of paint around the outside of your plate. Mix your first color in the middle of the plate. Use your paintbrush to spread out the color across a hand-sized area.

4. Gather your family members at your workspace.

5. Ask the oldest family member to place a hand down in the paint until it covers their entire handprint. Then press the hand firmly on the paper where it appears to be "growing" from the trunk.

6. Mix a bit of another color in the middle of the plate to change the handprint paint color.

7. Continuing from oldest to youngest, repeat steps 5 and 6 until each member of the family has added to the tree. (Tip: If there is room on your paper, have each family member print their other hand as well.)

8. Let the art dry.

9. Fill out and glue on the labels from the sheet of cardstock.

10. Ask each family member to sign their name near their handprint. Over time, check your grandkiddo's handprint to see how they've grown!

Paper Party Teacups

Plan a tea party together with these paper cups that *really* hold liquid!

4. Fold the bottom right corner across to match the other side.

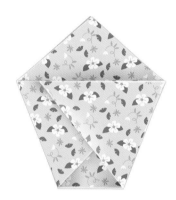

TIME TOGETHER: 30 min.

GATHER THESE ITEMS:

- 2 pieces of square paper (at least 8½" x 8½", or 21½ cm x 21½ cm)
- Drawing tools like crayons, colored pencils, or markers

5. Fold down the *front* top point, then flip over the cup.

LET'S GET STARTED:

1. Use your drawing tools to decorate one side of your paper.

2. Fold your paper in half to form a triangle, keeping your decorations on the outside, then place the long edge closest to you.

3. Pick up the bottom left corner and fold it across. The point of the fold should touch the other side to form a straight edge across the top.

6. Fold down the other top point. (This should leave an opening in the middle of the cup.)

7. Fold the flap across the top of the cup toward the right.

8. Unfold the flap, then fold it across the top of the cup toward the left.

9. Unfold the flap again. Press in on the 2 folds, and pinch in the middle to form a handle.

10. Flip the cup upside down and squeeze to round out the shape of the cup. Then fold in both bottom points toward the center to form the bottom of the cup.

11. Repeat steps 1 through 9 to fold your second teacup.

12. Fill them up—it's tea party time! Talk about your time together and any special memories you share.

Search and Find Collage

Make collage art featuring your favorite memories—
then play search and find!

TIME TOGETHER: **45 min.** **PLUS A FEW HOURS TO DRY**

GATHER THESE ITEMS:

- 1 large sheet of paper (at least 8½" x 11", or 21½ cm x 28 cm)
- 2 or more pieces of paper (any size)
- Glue
- 2 pairs of scissors—1 for you and 1 for your grandkiddo
- Magazines for cutting
- Drawing tools like crayons, colored pencils, or markers
- 2 or more index cards or small papers
- 2 or more pencils

LET'S GET STARTED:

1. Talk about your favorite things, places, and memories:

   ★ Look at the magazines together and cut out pictures that remind you of these favorites.

   ★ Use your smaller pieces of paper and drawing tools to draw some pictures, too, and cut them out.

2. Glue them onto your large sheet of paper. (Tip: Glue down the biggest pictures first and the smaller pictures last so that you can see them all in the finished collage.)

3. After the collage dries, give each person who helped an index card.

4. Write or draw 5 favorite things you see in the collage.

5. Switch cards, and search for the items written down on your new cards. Can you find them all?

CUT OUT LETTERS OR WORDS FOR YOUR COLLAGE—OR EVEN A SECRET MESSAGE!

Painted Leaf Patterns

Paint, roll, and print colorful leaf patterns together!

TIME TOGETHER: **45 min.**

PLUS A FEW HOURS TO DRY

GATHER THESE ITEMS:

- 10 or more leaves
- Paper (any color)
- Paper towels
- Rolling pin (or a can of food)
- Acrylic or tempera paint
- 2 or more paintbrushes
- Newspaper or other scrap paper
- Drawing tools like crayons, colored pencils, or markers

LET'S GET STARTED:

1. Go on a nature walk together and collect leaves of various types and sizes. Freshly fallen leaves work best for this craft.

2. Cover your work surface with newspaper.

3. Lay out a leaf flat in front of each of you. Paint one side of the leaf completely. (Tip: Paint either the bottom side of the leaf [with thicker veins] or the top side for different effects.)

4. Carefully place the leaf paint-side down on a sheet of paper. Lay down a paper towel on top of the leaf.

5. Take turns using the rolling pin to roll over the entire leaf, making sure to press hard as you roll.

6. Lift up the paper towel and peel up the leaf to see your print.

7. Create more patterns by stamping different painted leaves.

8. When the paint is dry, talk together to describe your artwork *and* your nature walk. What colors did you *see*? What textures did you *feel*? What sounds did you *hear*? Add drawings of these words and memories to your paper.

PLACE MULTIPLE PRINTS ON THE SAME SHEET OF PAPER TO CREATE A PATTERN! TRY FERNS, LONG GRASSES, AND PINE NEEDLES TO MAKE OTHER PRINTS!

Flowers that Last Forever

This vase full of flowers makes a great gift—
it never needs to be watered!

2. Touch the middle point of the triangle. One short side should have a solid seam and the other should have 8 edges of the paper. Fold the solid seam side across to line up with the long side.

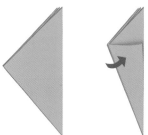

TIME TOGETHER: **30 min.**

GATHER THESE ITEMS:

☆ Cardstock from page 77
- Assorted colored sheets of square paper (larger sizes are easier to start with)
- Sheet of paper (at least 8½" x 11", or 21½ cm x 28 cm)
- 2 pairs of scissors—1 for you and 1 for your grandkiddo
- Pencil
- Glue

3. Cut off the top small triangle, right above the fold line.

4. Draw a rounded line from the top right corner toward the bottom point. Leave a space larger than your thumbprint at the bottom.

LET'S GET STARTED:

1. Choose a square of paper for each of you and fold them in half diagonally: 1, 2, 3 times.

5. Cut out the rounded shape along your drawn line.

30

6. Unfold the paper to reveal your flower.

7. Repeat steps 1 through 6 on a new square of paper.

8. Draw and cut out the shape of a vase from one of your extra squares of paper.

9. Cut out the flower centers, leaves, and decorations from the sheet of cardstock.

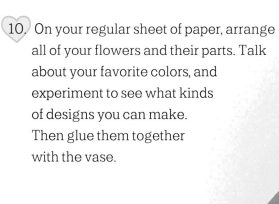

10. On your regular sheet of paper, arrange all of your flowers and their parts. Talk about your favorite colors, and experiment to see what kinds of designs you can make. Then glue them together with the vase.

11. When your art is dry, display your flowers to enjoy each day, or give them to someone you love so they can enjoy them.

USE A SQUARE PIECE OF NEWSPAPER, GRAPH PAPER, OR PAGES FROM MAGAZINES FOR ADDED TEXTURE, COLOR, AND VARIETY IN YOUR BOUQUET.

A Year of Memories

Turn beloved pieces of art into a calendar you can use all year long.

TIME TOGETHER: **45 min.**

GATHER THESE ITEMS:

 Cardstock from page 79
- Scissors
- Glue
- 12 handmade drawings or paintings (use collected art or make new pieces together)
- Hole punch
- Stick, chopstick, or skewer about 10" (25 cm) long
- String
- Optional: Paint and paintbrush

LET'S GET STARTED:

1. Cut out the 12 calendar strips from the sheet of cardstock.

2. Glue a calendar strip to each piece of art.

3. Order the art from January through December, and line up the top edges.

4. Punch 3 holes across the top, making sure they go through all 12 sheets. (If the paper is too thick, punch a few sheets at a time. Line up your holes through all 12 sheets.)

5. Cut 3 pieces of string, each about as long as your grandkiddo's hand.

6. Thread a string through the back of the middle hole, and pull through all 12 sheets.

7. Wrap the string once around the stick, then thread it back through the middle hole again. Secure the ends with tight knots on the back.

8. Repeat steps 6 and 7 with the next 2 pieces of string in the right and left holes.

9. Cut one more piece of string about as long as your grandkiddo's arm.

10. Tie an end of the string to each end of the stick.

11. Hang your calendar on a doorknob or hook and check off the days and months together!

PAINT YOUR STICK WITH STRIPES, DOTS, OR OTHER DESIGNS TO ADD MORE COLOR!

Let's Put On a Play

Create the props to put on a play about your favorite day.

GATHER THESE ITEMS:

 Cardstock from page 81
- Drawing tools like crayons, colored pencils, or markers
- A few sheets of cardstock or thick paper
- 2 pairs of scissors—1 for you and 1 for your grandkiddo
- Tape

LET'S GET STARTED:

1. Cut out the printed shapes, blank shapes, and holders from the cardstock. Also cut the slits in the bottoms of the shapes and the tops of the holders.

2. Talk about some favorite times you've spent together. Choose a memory that you'd both like to retell—it could be a birthday, a game you played together, a family tradition, or another time you both remember.

3. Think about the characters in your memory: Which people and animals were there? With your drawing tools, draw each character on one of the blank shapes. You can trim them to change the size, or use your extra paper to make more.

4. Think about other props that are important to retelling the memory. Did you unpack a suitcase? Eat an ice cream cone? Or play with a hula hoop? Draw each object on one of the blank shapes.

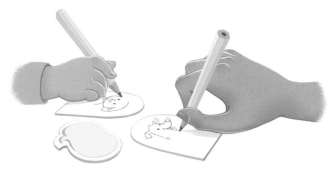

5. Press each character and prop into a holder so that it stands up.

6. Use your play pieces to act out your favorite memory! Create more props to tell other stories and memories, too.

DRAW THE SETTING FOR YOUR MEMORY ON AN EXTRA SHEET OF PAPER, OR MAKE A DIORAMA INSIDE A SHOEBOX!

Art for Your Arm

Make wearable art together with these folded paper bracelets.

GATHER THESE ITEMS:

- 2 drawings or paintings for cutting (or make some new ones just for this project) (Tip: They should be on regular-weight, 8½" x 11" [21½ cm x 28 cm] paper.)
- 2 pairs of scissors—1 for you and 1 for your grandkiddo
- Tape

2. Carefully fold the paper into thirds. Push hard on the folds to make crisp creases.

LET'S GET STARTED:

1. Fold your artwork in half like a book. Then fold it in half the other direction, into quarters.

3. Unfold the paper so you can see your 12 sections and cut them out along the fold lines.

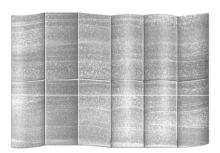

4. Repeat steps 1 through 3 with your second piece of art to create 24 sections in all.

5. Fold each strip in half the long way. Then fold again the other way.

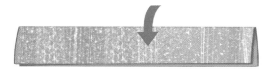

6. Place one strip inside the fold of the other.

7. Fold the front leg so that it is even with the other strip's bottom edge. Fold the same leg again over the top of the other strip.

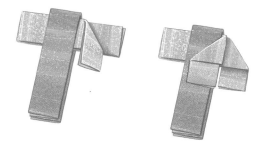

8. Flip over the strips and repeat step 7 with the other leg.

9. Use a small piece of tape to hold the 2 flaps in place.

10. Push up a new strip through the loop that you've made.

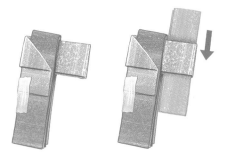

11. Repeat steps 6 and 7 to fold up the legs. This time, tuck both flaps into the pockets that were made by your first strip.

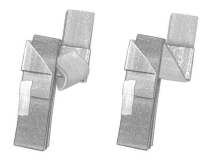

12. Repeat steps 9 and 10 to add, fold, and tuck more strips. When you've added about 15 strips, check the size on your wrist. Add more strips if you need the bracelet to be longer.

13. When the bracelet is complete, push the strip that you started with into your last loop. Fold and tuck in both legs.

14. Start the steps again to make a matching bracelet. Then wear your artwork together!

GLUE ON BEADS, SEQUINS, OR GLITTER FOR SOME EXTRA SPARKLE AND SHINE!

Handy Magnetic Art Holders

Hold on to these tiny hands to showcase your favorite art and treasures.

TIME TOGETHER: **30** min.

PLUS A FEW HOURS TO DRY

GATHER THESE ITEMS:

- Empty cereal box
- Pencil
- Acrylic or tempera paint
- Paintbrush
- Permanent marker
- Newspaper or other scrap paper
- Magnet tape (or 24 small, flat adhesive magnets)
- Scissors
- Optional: Artwork you've made together

LET'S GET STARTED:

1. Cover your workspace with newspaper.

2. Open up and flatten the seams of your cereal box with the plain side facing up.

3. Work together to trace each of your hands, one at a time, on the cereal box.
   (Tip: Avoid drawing over the seams of the box.)

4. Cut out the 4 traced hands.

5. Cover the handprints with paint.

6. When the handprints are dry, use the permanent marker to add fingernails, rings, other drawings, or written messages.

7. Cut 24 pieces from your magnet tape, each about the size of your fingerprint. (You can skip this step if you're using adhesive magnets.)

8. Peel off the protective backing and add the magnets to the back of each finger and one in the center of the palm.

9. Place the handprints on a magnetic surface to hold up other artwork you've made together.

Say "Hello" Pop-Up Card

Pop up to say hello to someone you love.

TIME TOGETHER: **30 min.**

GATHER THESE ITEMS:

- A photograph or home-drawn portrait of each of you
- 2 sheets of colored construction paper or cardstock
- Scissors
- Glue
- Drawing tools like crayons, colored pencils, or markers

4. Close the cut card and glue the edges of one face to the card with no cuts, like pages of a book inside the cover.

5. Glue the other face of the cut card and press it into the cover.

6. Cut out the people from your portraits.

7. Open up the card, then glue each picture on one side of the 2 pop-ups.

8. Decorate the rest of your card and add a message for the lucky friend or family member who will open it.

LET'S GET STARTED:

1. Fold both sheets of construction paper in half to form cards.

2. On one card, make 4 cuts as long as your finger along the fold.

3. Open up the cut card about halfway, then push the 2 middle cuts forward until the creases are *inside* the card.

THESE MAKE GREAT BIRTHDAY CARDS, TOO! ADD CUT-OUT PAPER BALLOONS TO THE PEOPLE IN THE PICTURES, OR CUT YOUR OWN CONFETTI TO PLACE INSIDE THE CARD.

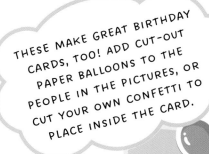

Playful Portraits

Use these tricks to draw side by side and create silly portraits together!

TIME TOGETHER: **15 min.**

GATHER THESE ITEMS:

- A few sheets of paper
- Drawing tools like crayons, colored pencils, or markers

LET'S GET STARTED:

1. Fold a sheet of paper in half 2 times so that you have 4 wide rectangle sections.

2. Start with your grandkiddo's playful portrait: Draw your grandkiddo's head in the top rectangle. Connect the head to the fold at the bottom of the rectangle. When you are done, fold the head back so that the next blank rectangle is on top. (Tip: The goal is to draw silly pictures collaboratively— try your best and add silly details as you go.)

3. Ask your grandkiddo to draw their torso on the next rectangle. Make sure it connects to the top and bottom folds. Have them fold it back to reveal the next blank rectangle.

4. When you grandkiddo passes it back, draw their legs, and make sure they connect to the top and bottom. Fold and pass back one last time.

5. To finish up the character, have your grandkiddo draw their feet in the last rectangle.

6. Unfold the paper and reveal what you've made together! (Tip: Talk together about the details you included—whether special or silly.)

7. Now make *your* playful portrait by switching roles so that your grandkiddo draws your head.

> GET CREATIVE— ADD WINGS, TIARAS, ANTLERS, JETPACKS, OR OTHER SILLY DETAILS!

Stitched Bookmarks

A stitch in time makes memories (and bookmarks!).

TIME TOGETHER: **45 min.**

GATHER THESE ITEMS:

- ☆ Cardstock from page 83
- • Hole punch
- • Yarn
- • 2 pairs of scissors—1 for you and 1 for your grandkiddo
- • Glue
- • Optional: 3 or more sheets of colorful cardstock

LET'S GET STARTED:

1. Cut out 2 bookmarks, 2 rolled paper needles, and 4 charms from the sheet of cardstock.

2. Punch holes on the markings in each cut piece.

3. Cut 2 pieces of yarn each about twice as long as your grandkiddo's arm.

4. Glue down the middle of one rolled paper needle. Place one end of a piece of yarn in the glue.

5. Tightly roll up the paper needle around the yarn.

6. Repeat steps 4 and 5 with your other rolled paper needle and piece of yarn.

7. Tie the end of a string to a charm, then repeat with the other string and another charm.

8. ♡ Stitch your bookmarks together. Use your paper needles to thread the yarn through the holes in the bookmarks. Your charms should hold the ends of the strings in place.

9. Cut off the paper needles once you're done with the bookmarks.

10. Tie on a second charm close to the bookmark. Then cut off the extra thread.

11. Mark the page of a favorite book you've read together!

Photo Heart Art

Sit side by side to talk about photographs of your favorite memories while you make this keepsake.

TIME TOGETHER: **45** min.

PLUS 30 MINUTES TO DRY

GATHER THESE ITEMS:

 Cardstock from page 85
- Large sheet of paper (the bigger the better)
- 20 or more photographs
- 2 pairs of scissors—1 for you and 1 for your grandkiddo
- Glue
- Pencil
- Drawing tools like crayons, colored pencils, or markers

LET'S GET STARTED:

1. Together, select 20 or more photographs of favorite memories, places, and people. Talk about when and where the photographs were taken.

2. Cut around the central focus of each photograph.

3. Lightly draw a large freehand heart shape in the middle of your paper with your pencil. (Don't worry if it isn't perfect! It will get covered up as you go.)

4. Lay down your biggest photographs first on the heart shape to create a border. Continue laying down more photos to fill in the inside of the shape, until all your photos have been used.

5. Move the photos around until they all fit into the heart shape. (Tip: If they don't all fit, or your heart shape isn't clear, try trimming your photographs a little smaller. Small photos work best!)

6. Add glue to the back of each photo, one at a time. Return each photo to its place until they are all glued.

7. Cut out the shapes from the sheet of cardstock. Write messages or draw pictures on them, then glue them to your heart.

8. Let the art dry. Then display it, frame it, or give it as a gift!

Lucky Stars

Catch a falling star together with this beautiful craft.

TIME TOGETHER: **45 min.**

GATHER THESE ITEMS:

- Sheet of paper or cardstock (any color or texture, 8½" x 11" [21½ cm x 28 cm] or larger)
- A photograph of your grandkiddo (holding their hands in the air if possible, but other poses will work, too)
- Glue
- Old magazine for cutting
- 2 pairs of scissors—1 for you and 1 for your grandkiddo
- Pencil

LET'S GET STARTED:

1. Cut out the outline of your grandkiddo from the photograph.

2. Add glue to the back of the photo and attach it to the bottom of your paper.

3. Flip through an old magazine together and collect 10 or more colors and textures that you both like, such as clouds, flowers, or wavy patterns. Rip out small pieces of the colors and textures, about the size of the palm of your hand.

4. Together, draw a star shape on the back of each pattern. Vary the sizes of the stars. Then cut them out.

5. Add glue to the back of each star.

6. Attach each star to the paper, as if your grandkiddo is throwing them in the air and the stars are floating above their head.

Playing with Memories

Create your own set of custom Memory tiles—then play the game together!

TIME TOGETHER: 30 min.

GATHER THESE ITEMS:

- ☆ Cardstock from page 87
- • Scissors
- • Drawing tools like crayons, colored pencils, or markers
- • Sheet of cardstock or thick paper
- • Glue
- ☆ "Use-anywhere stickers" from page 95

LET'S GET STARTED:

1. Cut out the Memory tiles from the cardstock on page 87.

2. Work together to decorate a pair of tiles: Choose a loved one and write their name on a tile each. Then each draw a picture of that same person. (Tip: Show something you love about them, or love to do with them! Include your favorite pets! Use stickers to add details.)

3. Repeat step 2 until all 8 pairs are done. Don't forget to make a pair of tiles featuring you, and another featuring your grandkiddo!

4. To store your game, fold your sheet of construction paper in half and then unfold it.

5. Fold each top corner in to meet in the middle.

6. Fold each side flap in about the width of your finger.

7. Fold the bottom half up until you can see just a triangle of the top of the flap.

8. Unfold it and add glue to the flaps above the crease. Fold the envelope shut and press on the seams.

9. Fold the top triangle down and wait for the envelope to dry.

10. Shuffle the tiles and place them facedown to play a game of Memory: The youngest player goes first and flips over 2 tiles. If they are a match, that player can pick them up and go again. If they are not a match, flip them back over and the turn is done. Take turns until all of the tiles have been picked up. The player with the most tiles wins.

11. Place the tiles inside your envelope to save for another round!

LEVEL UP YOUR GAME BY MAKING MORE TILES ON YOUR OWN CARDSTOCK!

Grandma and Me Dolls

Draw colorful outfits for each other in this twist on classic paper dolls.

TIME TOGETHER: **30** min.

GATHER THESE ITEMS:

- Sheet of paper
- A large round bowl or plate (the diameter should almost fill the paper)
- Pencil
- Drawing tools like crayons, colored pencils, or markers
- Scissors

LET'S GET STARTED:

1. Flip the bowl upside down on top of your paper.

2. Use a pencil to trace around the top of the bowl.

3. Cut out the traced circle from the paper.

4. Fold the paper in half 3 times, following these steps:

5. Use a pencil to draw half of a simple shape of yourself on one side. Your head should be toward the point of the paper. Help your grandkiddo draw a half-body shape on the other side. The pictures should join by holding hands.

6. Carefully cut along all the outlines. (This intricate cutting is easiest for an adult or an older grandkiddo.)

7. Unfold the paper dolls so they lay flat.

8. Draw and decorate together to make them look just like the two of you!

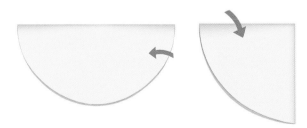

Butterfly Fingerprint Branch

Make butterflies as unique as your fingerprints that can land and stay all year long.

GATHER THESE ITEMS:

- A stick about the length of your arm
- Multicolored ink pad
- 2 or more sheets of light-colored paper
- Markers
- Glue

LET'S GET STARTED:

1. Help your grandkiddo to firmly press a thumb down on the ink pad.

2. Place the inked thumb on a sheet of paper to leave a thumbprint.

3. Work together to place 3 more prints in the shape of a butterfly.
   (Tip: Turn the paper to help each fingerprint face the correct direction.)

4. Practice a few more times together until your grandkiddo is ready to try making a butterfly on their own.

5. Use a different finger, a sheet of colored paper, or other colors of ink for more sizes, shapes, and colors of butterflies. Make a few butterflies with your own or another family member's fingerprints, too! Keep going until you've made 10 or more together.

6. Use markers to draw a body, head, and antennae on each butterfly. (Keep the antennae small and next to the head so that they will be easier to cut out.) Use markers to add extra colors to the wings, too.

7. Cut around each butterfly, being careful to keep the antennae intact.

8. Glue along the back of one butterfly, then press and hold it to the stick until it is securely attached.

9. Repeat step 8 for the rest of your butterflies.
   (Tip: Fold some butterflies in half to show them in a fluttering pose.)

10. Display the stick in a vase or jar to be surrounded by your very own butterflies.

Fall Thankfulness Garland

Preserve the fall season and the things you are thankful for together.

TIME TOGETHER:

60 min.

PLUS ABOUT A WEEK TO DRY

GATHER THESE ITEMS:

- 10 or more leaves
- 5 sheets of colorful paper
- 3 or more hardcover books
- 2 pairs of scissors—1 for you and 1 for your grandkiddo
- A large piece of wax paper
- Drawing tools like crayons, colored pencils, or markers
- Thread
- Needle

LET'S GET STARTED:

PRESS THE LEAVES

1. Go on a nature walk together and collect 10 or more leaves.

2. Lay each leaf on a sheet of colorful paper and trace around it, making sure that the outlines do not overlap.

3. Fold your wax paper in half and then open it back up so it lays flat.

4. Place all 10 real leaves onto the wax paper, and fold it closed so they lie flat inside.

5. Place your books on top of the wax paper. Now don't touch! (You can skip ahead and make the garland while you wait.)

6. Wait about a week before checking if the leaves are dry. If they are not, put the books back on top of the wax paper and wait another few days.

MAKE THE GARLAND

1. While you wait for the leaves to dry, cut out the leaves you traced on the paper.

2. Talk about things you are each thankful for and write one on each leaf, then place them in a safe space until your real leaves are dried.

3. When the real leaves are dried, thread the needle, then carefully push it twice through a real leaf.

4. Next, push the needle twice through a paper leaf.

5. Repeat steps 3 and 4 to make a pattern of real leaves and paper leaves.

6. When all the leaves are on the thread, gently move them right or left to arrange your garland.

7. Hang your finished garland of leaves as a reminder of the things you are both thankful for!

Hands Down Best Wreath

Helping hands can create the best wreath in town.

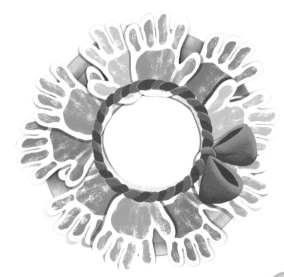

TIME TOGETHER: **45 min.** PLUS A FEW HOURS TO DRY

GATHER THESE ITEMS:

- Several sheets of paper (8½" x 11" [21½ cm x 28 cm] or larger, any color)
- Washable paint (finger paint or tempera) in various colors
- Paintbrush
- Large plate or tray
- 2 pairs of scissors—1 for you and 1 for your grandkiddo
- Paper plate (a large, thick one is best)
- Glue
- Optional: Ribbon or bow

LET'S GET STARTED:

1. Place a few dollops of various colors of paint around the outside of your plate. Use the paintbrush to mix your first color (or a swirl of colors) in the middle of the plate. (Tip: Choose colors to match your season!)

2. Roll up your sleeves. Take turns with your grandkiddo: Place a hand down in the paint until it covers the entire handprint. Then press it firmly in the center of a sheet of paper. Keep going, using additional sheets of paper as needed, until you have about 20 handprints in all.

3. Leave the paint to dry for a few hours or overnight.

4. Cut around the rough shape of each handprint.

5. Poke your scissors through the center of the plate and cut out a hole. The remaining ring should be 2" or 3" (5 cm or 7½ cm) thick.

6. Glue the handprints around the wreath until the plate is covered.

7. Hang the wreath to display your handiwork!

ADD A RIBBON OR A BOW!

Shadow Play

Create your own shadow puppets to tell the story of your dream day together!

TIME TOGETHER: 45 min.

GATHER THESE ITEMS:

 Cardstock from page 89
- 6 or more pencils or chopsticks
- 2 pairs of scissors—1 for you and 1 for your grandkiddo
- Tape
- Flashlight or desk lamp

LET'S GET STARTED:

1. Talk and dream together: If you could go anywhere together and do anything you wanted, where would you go and what would you do?

2. Cut out the puppet pieces from the cardstock and play! Combine the shapes together on a table to see what you can make.

3. Tape the puzzle pieces together into the characters that you need for your story. (Tip: When you make shadows, only the SHAPE will matter.) Add accessories like hats, wings, and more. Remember to make a character for each of you!

4. Make a setting. Are there mountains? A playground? A beach?

5. Tape each puppet to its own pencil.

6. Dim or turn off the lights in the room. Place your flashlight or desk lamp so that it points against a wall.

7. Hold your puppets between the light and the wall to make shadows, then tell the story of your dream day with their shadows!

All at Home

Create a house and fill it with photos of your friends and family!

TIME TOGETHER: **45 min.** PLUS A FEW HOURS TO DRY

GATHER THESE ITEMS:

- Empty half-gallon (liter) milk carton
- 2 pairs of scissors—1 for you and 1 for your grandkiddo
- Glue
- Tape
- A few photographs or home-drawn portraits of your family
- 2 sheets of colored construction paper
- Drawing tools like crayons, colored pencils, or markers

LET'S GET STARTED:

1. Cut off the top flap of your milk carton.

2. Lay the carton on its side, then mark the width of the top on a piece of construction paper.

3. Fold the paper evenly on the line to make a rectangle. Then cut out the rectangle along the fold line.

4. Fold the rectangle in half and glue it on top of the milk carton, like a roof. (If it hangs off more than you like, trim it with scissors.)

IF YOUR CARTON HAS A PLASTIC POURING SPOUT, LEAVE IT AS A CHIMNEY OR REMOVE THE LID AND PUSH THE REMAINING PLASTIC INSIDE.

5. Lay the carton on its side on your other piece of construction paper, then mark the height of the carton on the short end.

6. Fold the paper evenly on the traced line. Then cut along the fold.

7. Wrap the larger piece of the paper around the milk carton. Then crease the corners, and hold it temporarily in place with 2 pieces of tape. (This will cover 3 sides. The uncovered side can be the back of the house, or cut out a piece of paper large enough to cover it.)

8. Draw windows and doors on all 3 sides.

9. Gently take off the tape, then lay the paper flat.

10. Cut out each door on 3 sides, leaving one long side attached. Then fold open each door.

11. Cut out each window entirely, or leave one side attached and fold them open.

12. Together, choose the people in your photographs that you'd like to feature in each window and door.

Tape your pictures to the back of the paper so that you see them when you open the windows and doors from the front.

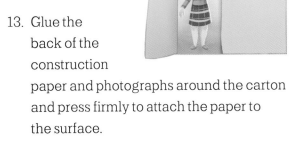

13. Glue the back of the construction paper and photographs around the carton and press firmly to attach the paper to the surface.

14. Draw details on the outside of the house, such as trees, flowers, or a pet.

15. Display your art to remember your memories of being all together.

Painting with Paper

Work side by side to make art—
by painting with paper!

2. Cut out and tear shapes of various colors from the tissue paper.

3. Together, play with the colors and shapes: Plan out and lay the tissue paper pieces onto your watercolor papers. Make pictures, letters, or just abstract designs. (Tip: Crumple the tissue paper for a neat effect!)

TIME TOGETHER: 45 min.

PLUS A FEW HOURS TO DRY

GATHER THESE ITEMS:

- Bleeding tissue paper in multiple colors (bleeding tissue paper is different from regular tissue paper, and can be found at craft stores or online)
- 2 or more sheets of watercolor paper
- 2 pairs of scissors—1 for you and 1 for your grandkiddo
- Spray bottle filled with water
- Newspaper or other scrap paper
- Optional: Disposable gloves

LET'S GET STARTED:

1. Cover your workspace with newspaper.

4. When your designs are ready, lightly but thoroughly spray both papers with your spray bottle. Adjust the tissue paper with your fingers if any of the pieces move. (Be careful! The dye from the tissue paper may stain your fingers, so wash your hands frequently or wear disposable gloves.)

5. Allow the papers to dry for a few hours. Then peel up the tissue paper pieces and throw them away, revealing your beautiful "paintings" underneath.

6. Write a message on top of the colors to make a poster. Or fold the paper in half and write on the inside to make a card. Display or share your colorful creations!

Secret Message Origami Hearts

Fill up your hearts with these folded paper decorations.

TIME TOGETHER: **15 min.**

GATHER THESE ITEMS:

- 2 pieces of square paper (8½" [21½ cm] square or larger)
- 2 small strips of paper
- Writing tool like a pencil, pen, or marker

LET'S GET STARTED:

1. Make your hearts together: Fold each paper in half like a book, then unfold the sheets so they lie flat.

2. Fold up a small strip along the bottom of your papers—about as wide as a finger.

3. Fold the new bottom edges to the tops of the sheets and crease them firmly.

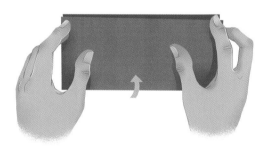

4. Fold down the right corners to the bottom edges. Repeat this with the left corners.

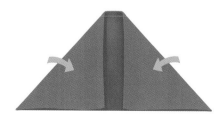

5. Fold up the bottom right corners. The tops of the folds should align with the bottoms of your papers, and the points should match the ends of your flaps, like the picture.

6. Repeat step 5 with the bottom left corners of each paper.

7. Fold up and crease your 2 bottom flaps.

8. Unfold the flaps and tuck them inside the pockets.

9. Fold in and crease the 4 tabs on each heart, where shown.

10. Pick up your heart in your hands. Find the small hole in the bottom and blow into it! Your heart should puff up. (Tip: If it doesn't puff up fully, use your fingers to press the paper out from the inside.)

11. Hold your heart in one hand and use your other hand to form the top of the shape into the heart.

12. Write a message on your strip of paper. Fold and roll it up small, so that it fits into the hole in the bottom of the heart. Slip the message inside and give your secret message heart to someone you love!

Giant 3-D Snowflakes

Let it snow anytime with these paper snowflakes made with love. Every snowflake is unique, just like you.

TIME TOGETHER: **45 min.**

GATHER THESE ITEMS:

- 6 pieces of equally sized square paper (around 6" to 8" [15 cm to 21½ cm] square works well)
- Scissors
- Clear tape
- Optional: String for hanging

LET'S GET STARTED:

1. Fold a square paper in half to form a triangle. Then fold it in half again to make a smaller triangle.

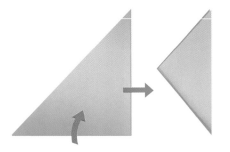

2. Make 3 cuts on a short side of the triangle, but stop the cuts before they reach the other short side.

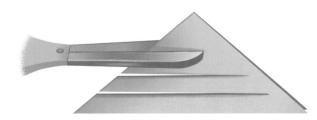

3. Unfold the paper so it lays flat. Wrap the 2 innermost triangles around your grandkiddo's finger and tape the pieces together.

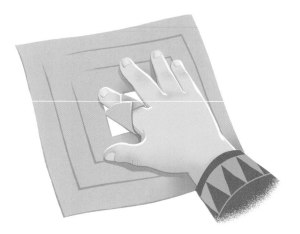

4. Flip over the whole paper. Wrap the next 2 smallest triangles around your grandkiddo's finger, then tape the pieces together.

5. Repeat this step 2 more times by flipping and taping until all the triangles are secured.

6. Repeat steps 1 through 5 with the remaining square sheets of paper.

7. Place your 6 constructed pieces in a circle to form a snowflake. Tape each piece to the one next to it in the middle and at the widest part.

8. Display your giant snowflake. Share together: Is it snowing where you live now? Has it *ever* snowed there? What is your favorite thing to play in the snow? (Or what do you want to try next time you see snow?)

USE 6 SMALLER OR 6 LARGER SQUARES OF PAPER TO MAKE SNOWFLAKES OF DIFFERENT SIZES, THEN STRING THEM UP AS A BANNER!

Grandma and Me Journal

Create a record of your thoughts, dreams, jokes, and time together.

TIME TOGETHER: 60 min.

GATHER THESE ITEMS:

 Cardstock from page 91
- Large empty cereal box
- Pencil
- 9 sheets of light-colored paper
- Drawing tools like crayons, colored pencils, or markers
- 2 pairs of scissors—1 for you and 1 for your grandkiddo
- Hole punch
- A piece of yarn or string about 4 times as long as your grandkiddo's arm
- Glue
- Optional: Acrylic or tempera paint, paintbrush

LET'S GET STARTED:

1. Open up the seams of your cereal box until it lies flat. Place a sheet of paper in the middle of the flat box (avoiding seams) and trace around it with a pencil.

2. Cut out the traced rectangle and fold it in half to make your journal cover.

3. Decorate and draw on your cover: Use drawing tools on the plain side, or paint on the printed side. (Tip: If you chose paint, let the cover dry before going to the next step.)

4. Place the hole punch over the top end of the crease and create a hole, then repeat on the bottom end of the crease.

5. Line up and fold in half 3 sheets of your paper. Press hard on the thick crease to make a crisp edge. Repeat with the other pages, so that you have 3 folded sets of 3 pages each.

6. In one stack, place your hole punch over 1 end of the crease and create a hole, then repeat on the other end. Repeat with the other 2 stacks.

7. Line up all 3 stacks and start binding your journal: Take one end of your string and pull about half of your string through the top-right hole.

8. Follow the path: Weave inside the stack, down, inside the stack, down, inside the stack, and out the bottom left. Pull tight.

9. Take the string in the upper right and follow the next path: down, inside the stack, down, inside the stack, and out the bottom right. Pull tight.

10. Line up your stacks in the cover and pull each string through the closest hole.

11. From the outside, pull each string up or down the spine and in the other hole. Both strings are now on the inside. Pull them into a tight knot and trim the ends.

12. Cut out the journal prompts from your sheet of cardstock. Read the prompts on both sides, choose the ones that you like best, and glue them at the tops of the pages. (Or, write your own prompts!)

13. Fill in the journal together!

Remember Today Time Capsule

TIME TOGETHER: **60 min.**

Time flies! Record the details of today so you can revisit the memories any time you want.

GATHER THESE ITEMS:

☆ Cardstock from page 93
- Drawing tools like crayons, colored pencils, or markers
- 6 sheets of colorful paper
- Large manila envelope
- Ribbon or string
- 2 pairs of scissors—1 for you and 1 for your grandkiddo
- Glue

LET'S GET STARTED:

1. Draw on and decorate your manila envelope.

2. Cut out the time capsule labels and prompts from your sheet of cardstock.

3. Ask your grandkiddo to stand up tall. Hold the ribbon up high next to them until it touches the ground, then cut the piece where it marks the height of your grandkiddo.

4. With your grandkiddo's help, cut a second piece of ribbon to mark your own height. (Tip: While you probably won't grow, it will be fun to see how much closer your heights get as your grandkiddo grows!)

5. Trace and cut out each of your right hands on a piece of colorful paper.

6. Glue the hands together with the palms aligned at the bottom, facing the same direction.

7. Record your thoughts: Fold 2 pieces of paper into quarters (1 for you and 1 for your grandkiddo).

8. Glue a cut-out prompt on each of the 4 boxes. Then use your drawing tools to respond to the prompts, sharing aloud as you go.

9. Fold and then unfold 2 new pieces of paper in half (one for you and one for your grandkiddo).

10. Glue labels onto the top and bottom boxes. Then use your drawing tools to respond, sharing aloud as you go.

GRANDMA

11. When you are done, place all your recordings and responses into the time capsule. (Tip: Add any other crafts from this book that you'd like to save for the future!) Write the date on the seal, then glue it on to close the envelope.

12. Open and share your time capsule sometime in the future. How long can you wait?

TIME CAPSULE

Odd Dot

Odd Dot is a registered trademark of Macmillan Publishing Group, LLC

120 Broadway, New York, New York 10271

OddDot.com

COVER DESIGNER Christina Quintero

TITLE LETTERING Kate Avino

INTERIOR DESIGNER Kayleigh McCann

EDITOR Kate Avino

ISBN 978-1-250-80413-6

Our books may be purchased in bulk for promotional, educational, or business use. Please contact your local bookseller or the Macmillan Corporate and Premium Sales Department at (800) 221-7945 ext. 5442 or by e-mail at MacmillanSpecialMarkets@macmillan.com.

First edition, 2022

Printed in China by RR Donnelley Asia Printing Solutions Ltd.,
Dongguan City, Guangdong Province

1 3 5 7 9 10 8 6 4 2

Together Forever Jar

Love You Everywhere Guidepost

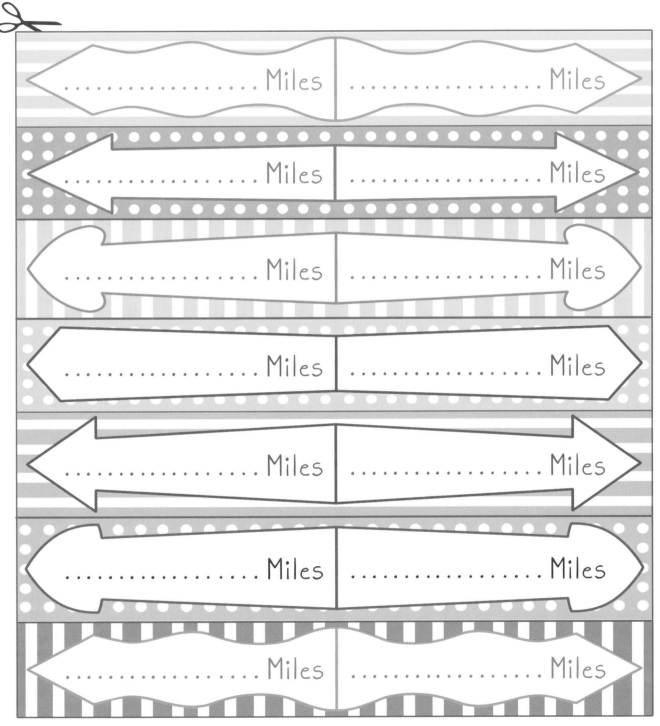

Miles

Miles

Miles

Miles

Miles

Miles

Miles

Miles

Miles

Miles

Miles

Miles

Miles

Miles

Mini Notes to Cherish: Instructions on page **12**

To
from

To
from

To
from

To
from

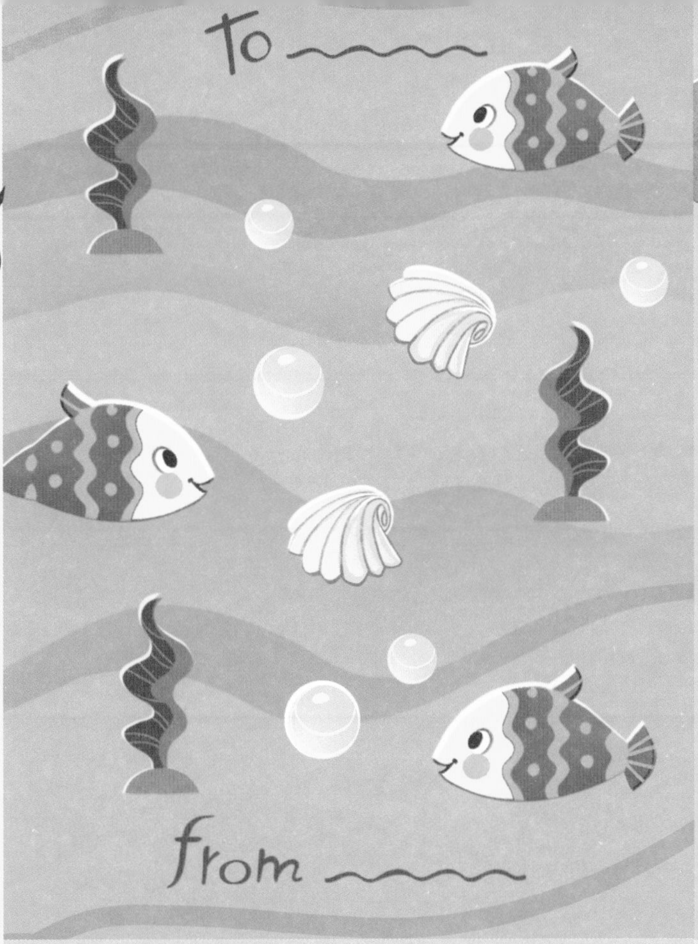

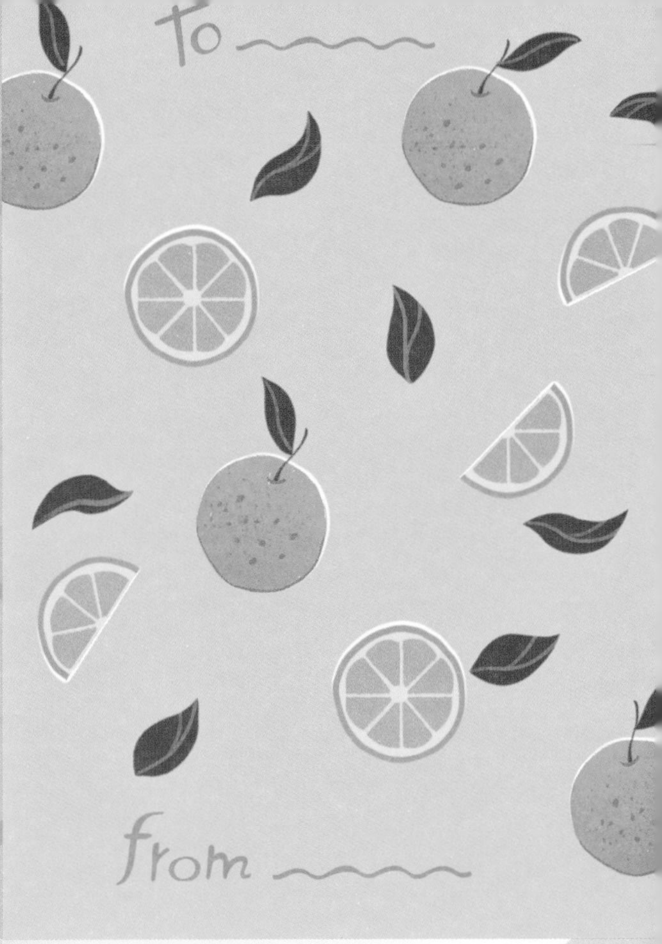

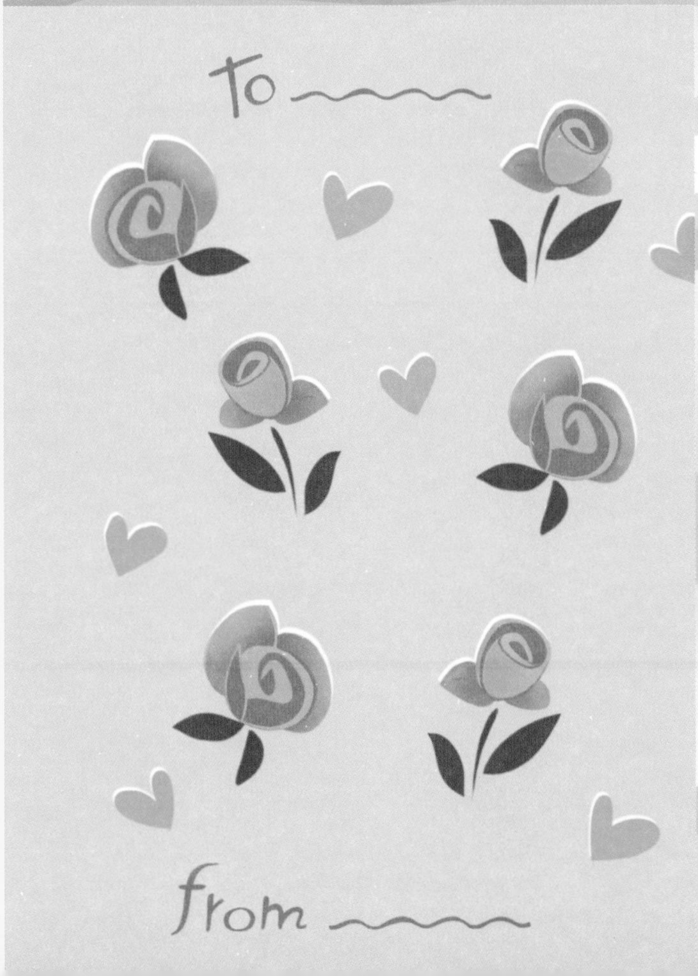

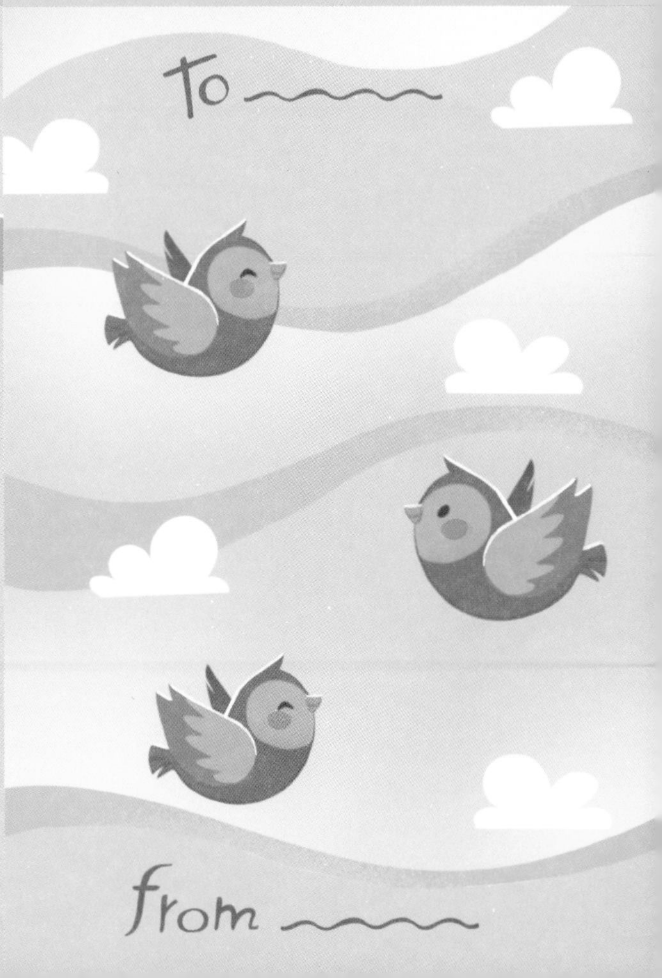

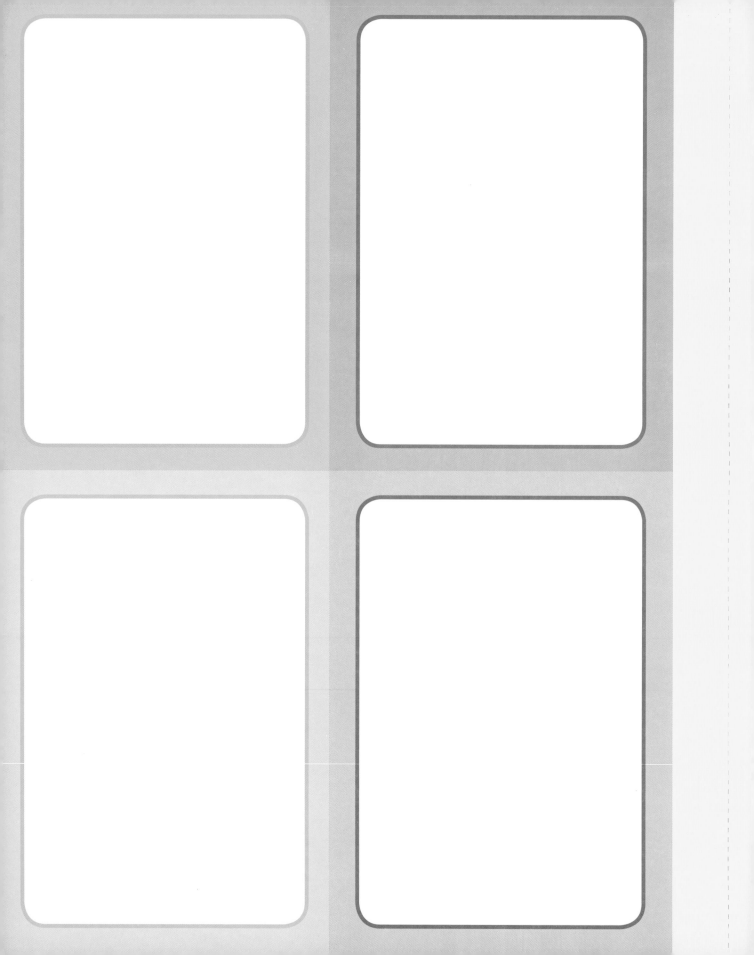

Rolling Conversations

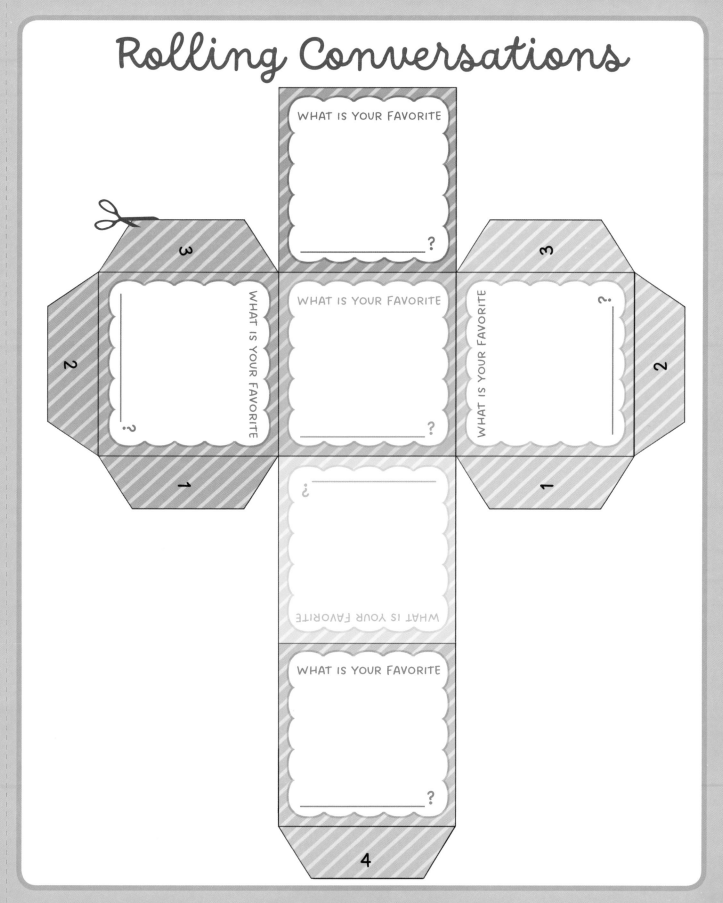

WHAT IS YOUR FAVORITE

_____ ?

WHAT IS YOUR FAVORITE

_____ ?

WHAT IS YOUR FAVORITE

_____ ?

WHAT IS YOUR FAVORITE

? _____

WHAT IS YOUR FAVORITE

? _____

WHAT IS YOUR FAVORITE

_____ ?

Favorite Things
Pencil Toppers

Treasure Pockets: Instructions on page **21**

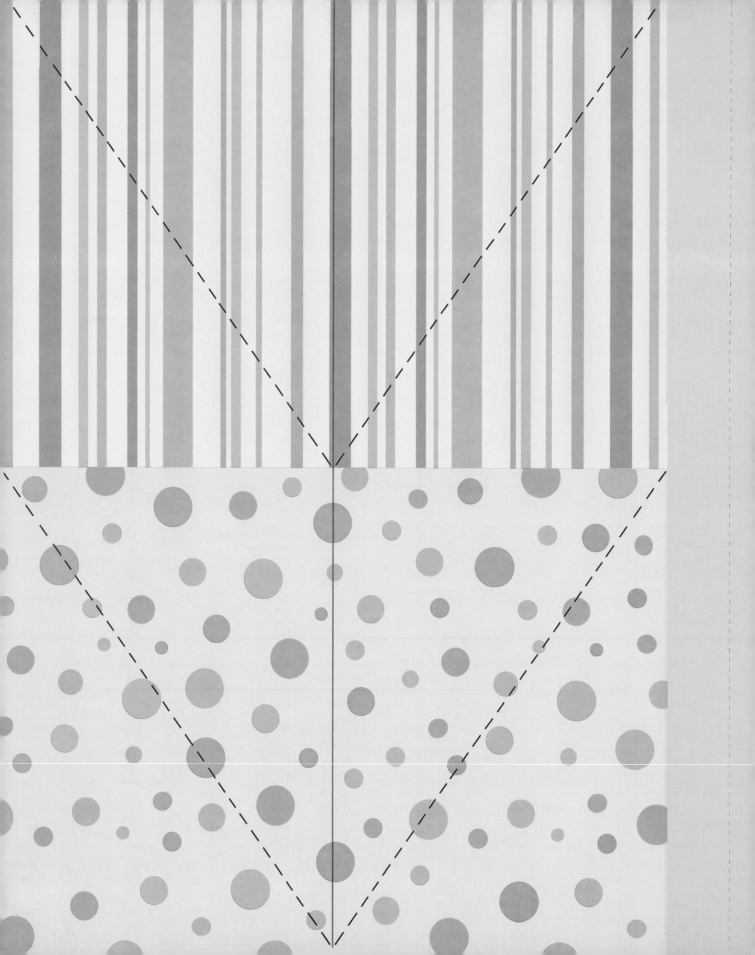

Our Family Tree

MADE with love by:

DATE:

Flowers that Last Forever

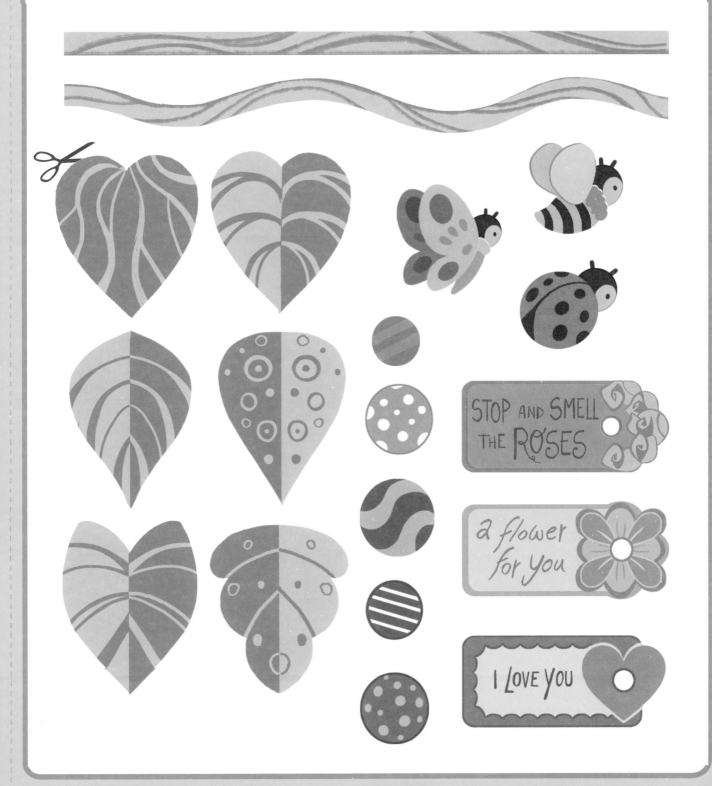

STOP AND SMELL THE ROSES

a flower for you

I LOVE YOU

JANUARY	FEBRUARY	MARCH	APRIL	MAY	JUNE	JULY	AUGUST	SEPTEMBER	OCTOBER	NOVEMBER	DECEMBER
1	1	1	1	1	1	1	1	1	1	1	1
2	2	2	2	2	2	2	2	2	2	2	2
3	3	3	3	3	3	3	3	3	3	3	3
4	4	4	4	4	4	4	4	4	4	4	4
5	5	5	5	5	5	5	5	5	5	5	5
6	6	6	6	6	6	6	6	6	6	6	6
7	7	7	7	7	7	7	7	7	7	7	7
8	8	8	8	8	8	8	8	8	8	8	8
9	9	9	9	9	9	9	9	9	9	9	9
10	10	10	10	10	10	10	10	10	10	10	10
11	11	11	11	11	11	11	11	11	11	11	11
12	12	12	12	12	12	12	12	12	12	12	12
13	13	13	13	13	13	13	13	13	13	13	13
14	14	14	14	14	14	14	14	14	14	14	14
15	15	15	15	15	15	15	15	15	15	15	15
16	16	16	16	16	16	16	16	16	16	16	16
17	17	17	17	17	17	17	17	17	17	17	17
18	18	18	18	18	18	18	18	18	18	18	18
19	19	19	19	19	19	19	19	19	19	19	19
20	20	20	20	20	20	20	20	20	20	20	20
21	21	21	21	21	21	21	21	21	21	21	21
22	22	22	22	22	22	22	22	22	22	22	22
23	23	23	23	23	23	23	23	23	23	23	23
24	24	24	24	24	24	24	24	24	24	24	24
25	25	25	25	25	25	25	25	25	25	25	25
26	26	26	26	26	26	26	26	26	26	26	26
27	27	27	27	27	27	27	27	27	27	27	27
28	28	28	28	28	28	28	28	28	28	28	28
29	29	29	29	29	29	29	29	29	29	29	29
30		30	30	30	30	30	30	30	30	30	30
31		31		31		31	31		31		31

Draw your own scene:

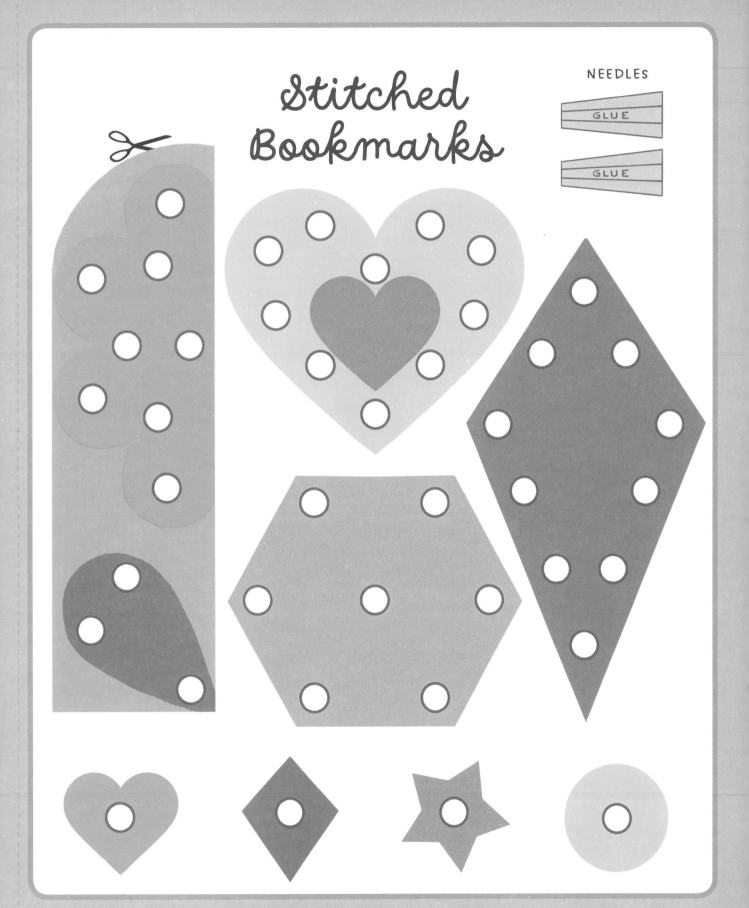

Photo Heart Art

Playing with Memories

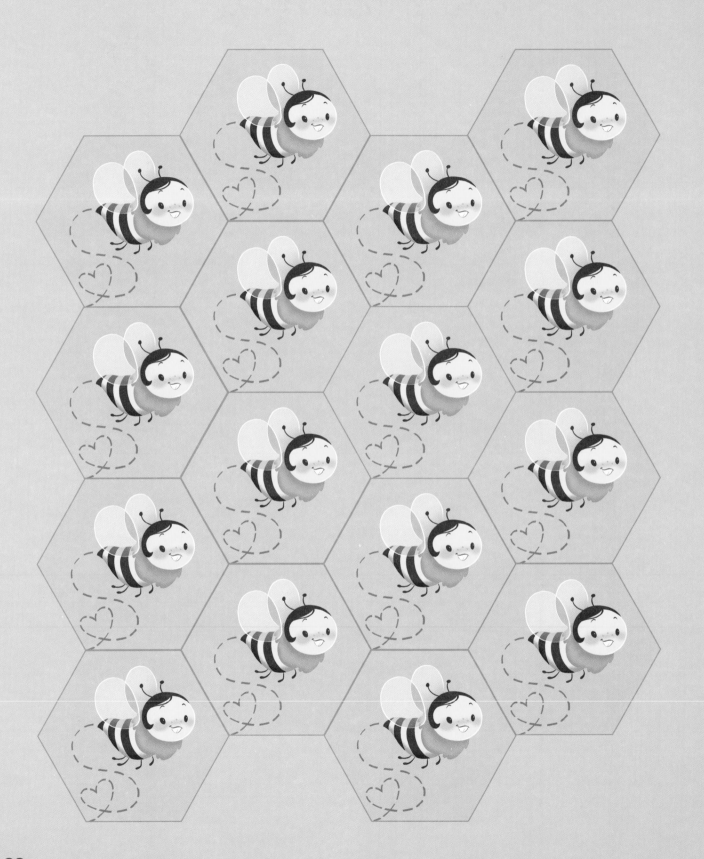

Shadow Play

If you could invent a new fruit, what would it look and taste like?

DATE:

If you could have 1 secret way to explore-swim deep underwater, fly, or tunnel underground-which would you choose?

DATE:

What toppings would you put on the ultimate bowl of ice cream?

DATE:

If you could travel to 1 place in outer space, where would it be?

DATE:

What would your dream treehouse look like?

DATE:

Share a memory of a time someone was kind to you.

DATE:

What would your dream houseboat look like?

DATE:

Share a memory of a time you were kind to someone.

DATE:

If you could have any animal for a pet, what would it be?

DATE:

If you could shrink down to the size of your thumb for 1 day, where would you explore?

DATE:

What are your 3 favorite things that are the color yellow?

DATE:

If you could talk to animals or plants, which would you choose? What would you ask?

DATE:

What was your favorite part of your last birthday?

DATE:

What is your favorite animal? Why is it your favorite?

DATE:

If you could design your own birthday cake to be any size, shape, and design, what would it look like?

DATE:

What would your dream flying car look like?

DATE:

If you could have 3 super powers, what would they be?

DATE:

If you could be any animal for 1 day, which would you be? Where would you go?

DATE:

If you could learn 1 new skill overnight, what would it be?

DATE:

What are your 3 favorite things that are the color red?

DATE:

If you could design your own rollercoaster, what would it look like?

DATE:

If you could change the sound that thunder makes, what would it sound like? How would your family react to the new sound?

DATE:

What would your dream robot look like? What would it be able to do?

DATE:

What do you think is the best job in the whole world?

DATE:

If you were going on a trip to the jungle, what would you pack?

DATE:

Imagine that you fell into a magical puddle and kept going down, down, down. Where would you go?

DATE:

What is 1 thing you are thankful for today?

DATE:

If you could change your hair to look like anything you wanted—any color, any accessories, any special tricks, any length—what would you choose?

DATE:

If you could spend a day taming dragons or chasing rainbows, which would you choose?

DATE:

If you could have a pet fly or pet shark, which would you choose?

DATE:

What is your favorite holiday? What do you like to do to celebrate?

DATE:

If you could design a new firework, what would it be like?

DATE:

Remember Today Time Capsule

I'M HERE TO HOLD YOUR HAND!

WHEN YOU FIRST SAW YOUR GRANDKIDDO TODAY, WHAT DID YOU SAY OR DO?

WHEN YOU FIRST SAW YOUR GRANDMA TODAY, WHAT DID YOU SAY OR DO?

IF YOU COULD GO ANYWHERE TOGETHER TODAY, WHERE WOULD IT BE?

IF YOU COULD GO ANYWHERE TOGETHER TODAY, WHERE WOULD IT BE?

WHAT IS YOUR FAVORITE FOOD TO MAKE AND EAT TOGETHER?

WHAT IS YOUR FAVORITE FOOD TO MAKE AND EAT TOGETHER?

WHAT IS YOUR FAVORITE GAME TO PLAY TOGETHER?

WHAT IS YOUR FAVORITE GAME TO PLAY TOGETHER?

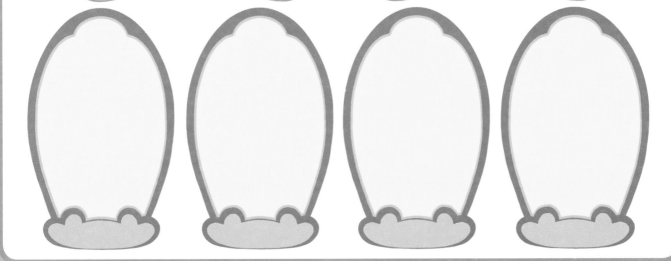